I KNOW FORWARD AND BACKWARD

By Rosie Banks

Gareth Stevens
PUBLISHING

first concepts

Directions tell us which way.

Forward and backward are directions.

The dog looks forward.

The dog looks backward.

The girl swings forward.

11

The girl swings backward.

13

The boy jumps forward.

15

The boy jumps
backward.

17

The dancer bends forward.

19

The dancer bends backward.

21

We can move forward
and backward too!